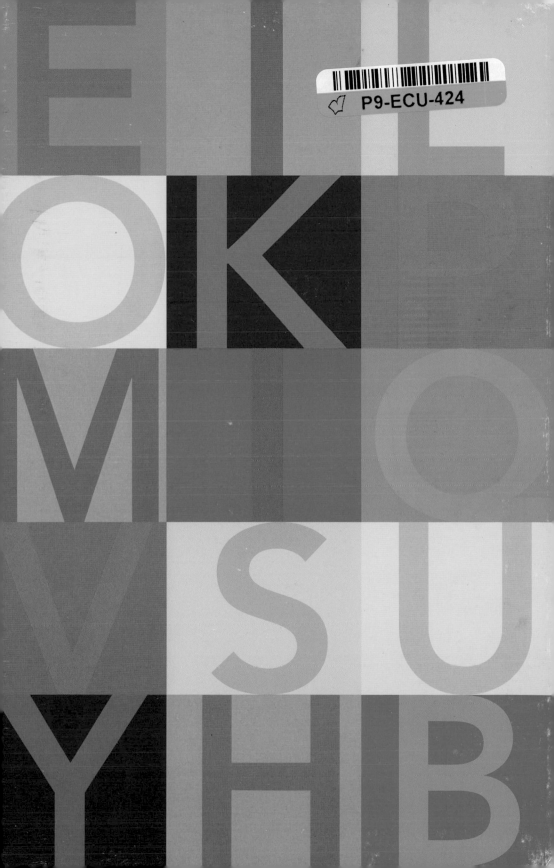

Dear Parents,

Is your child a new reader? If yes, one good way to help your child build confidence and word recognition skills is by introducing word families.

The die-cuts at the bottoms of the pages draw attention to three different word families (letters show through each die-cut shape).

Once your child can read "**og**", then he or she can focus on the beginning letters and sounds:

> **h**og, **j**og, **f**og, **b**og

After the single words are learned, the pictures help your child read the words in phrases:

> **frog jogs** **frog and hog in the fog**
> **frog on hog**

It's much easier to learn a group of words than to memorize them by sight one word at a time. A sight vocabulary is limited by the number of words that can be held in memory.

Recognizing words by families hugely increases the number of words that your child can know. It gives your child a way to sound out new words (reading specialists call these "word attack" skills), thereby increasing the likelihood he or she will feel successful.

Help your child with the 25 new words in this book by giving him or her multiple chances to read it until all the words are mastered.

Most important, have fun together!

Harriet Ziefert, M.A.
Language Arts/Reading Specialist

Jog

by **Harriet Ziefert**

Illustrated by **Yukiko Kido**

flip-a

WORD

Word Families

The world is full of print. Written words are everywhere. It's impossible to learn printed words by memorizing them word, by word, by word. To make learning easier, words can be grouped into families.

The words in a word family have two or more letters that are the same. We read "og" words and "all" words, "eat" words and "op" words. If you know "eat," then it's easier to learn beat, heat, and meat.

This book has words from three different word families. All the words in a family rhyme—which means you can add other words to the group by changing the first letter.

It's okay if some of the words you think of are not real words. If you make "deat" or "reat" or "zeat," it's not wrong— as long as you know the difference between a real word and a nonsense word.

Flip each page and presto-change-o— a new word appears!

The

og

Family

c
n
k
m
g
p
h
r
d
s
w

frog

h

j

fog

frog on hog

frog jogs

frog and hog in the fog

frog jogs in the fog

The
all
Family

f l w m g n b r d w t

ball

W

small

ball on a wall

tall wall

small ball on a tall wall

The
eat
Family

f

l

w

m

g

n

b

r

d

w

t

eat

m

h

treat

eat the meat

eat the treat

heat the meat

eat the meat and the treat

The og Family

frog	bog
hog	log
jog	fog

The all Family

ball	small
wall	fall
tall	hall
mall	

The eat Family

eat	beat
meat	neat
heat	seat
treat	

Find the words in each family.

ball hog eat

neat tall jog

log

seat frog treat dog

wall meat bog mall

dog hall eat heat

beat

stop treat wall

log seat

jog fog ball

small neat sun

fall tall frog

hog

Word Family Activities

- Choose two words from the word family and make your own "flip-a-word" illustrations. Remember to make a cut-out at the bottom of the page where the word family shows through.

- Words in a word family rhyme. Learn a song or a poem that rhymes and share it. Or read a book that rhymes and guess which words rhyme.

- Write or tell or draw a story using two or three of the characters in this book. What happens next?

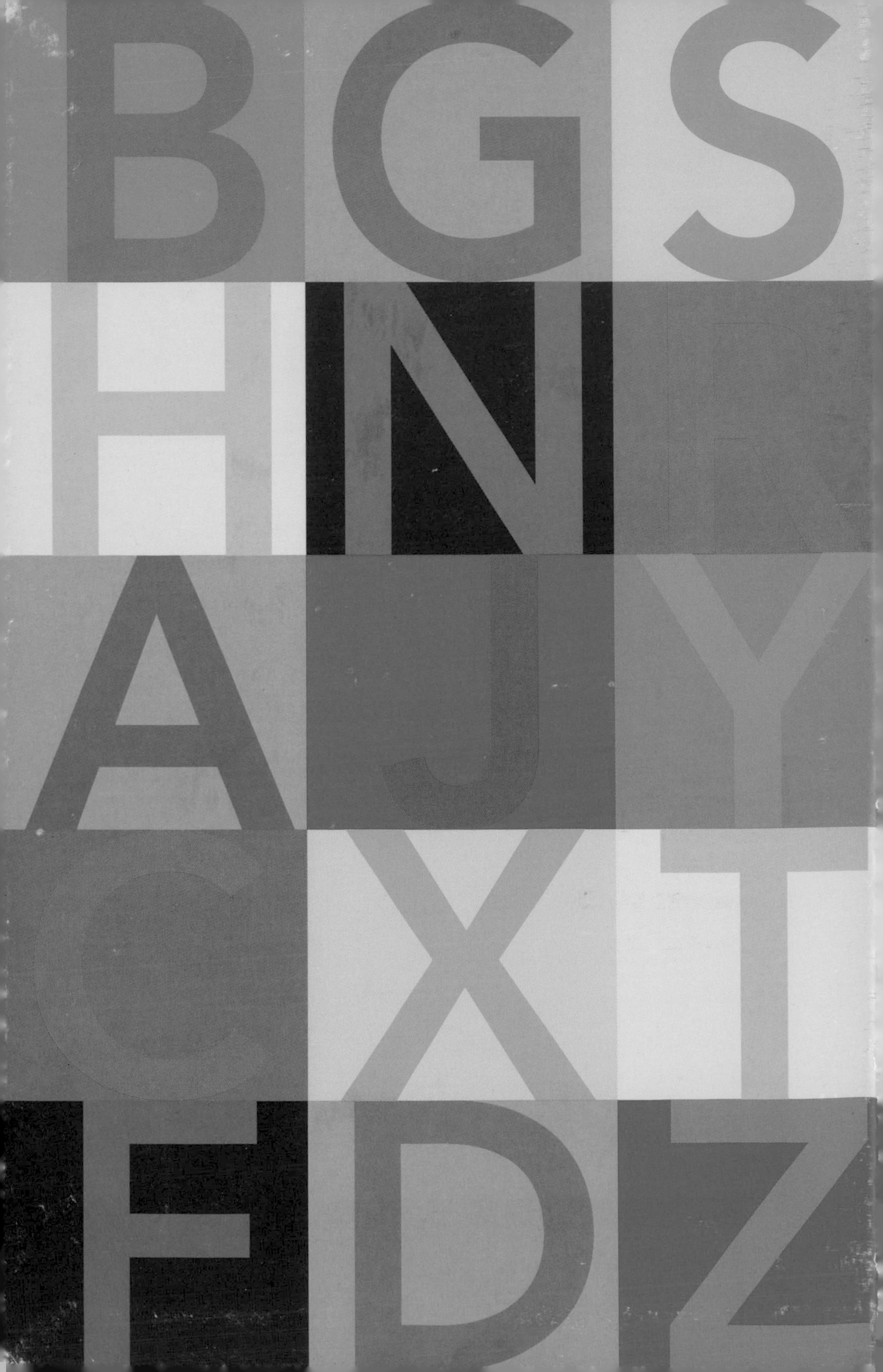
BGS
HNR
AJY
CXT
FDZ